Professional Success

ISRAEL J. ABIFARIN

Copyright © 2024 Israel J. Abifarin All rights reserved

The characters and events portrayed in this book are fictitious. Any similarity to real persons, living or dead, is coincidental and not intended by the author.

No part of this book may be reproduced, or stored in a retrieval system, or transmitted in any form or by any means, electronic, mechanical, photocopying, recording, or otherwise, without express written permission of the publisher.

ISBN: 9798343325836

DEDICATION

This book is dedicated to GOD first.
And to all the professionals striving for growth, mastery, and success—this book is for you. Also to the mentors and leaders whose guidance lights the way, your impact goes beyond what you'll ever know

CONTENTS

INTRODUCTION..1

DEFINING PROFESSIONAL SUCCESS............................5

SKILL DEVELOPMENT...15

BUILDING MEANINGFUL RELATIONSHIPS..................33

TAKING CONTROL OF YOUR CAREER........................41

CONCLUSION..55

INTRODUCTION

It was at a mentor's retirement party that the idea for this book was born.

The event was for a mentor of mine, someone whose career had left an indelible mark on everyone in the room. As I walked through the crowd that evening, I couldn't help but notice the mix of faces—some older, reminiscing about the "old days" of their careers, and others younger, wide-eyed and eager, full of ambition and curiosity. But there was one thing that stood out to me: no matter their age, everyone had immense respect for this man—a professional who embodied success in every sense of the word.

This mentor had not just **succeeded in his profession**; he had mastered it. He had built meaningful relationships, refined his skills over the years, and most importantly, he had taken ownership of his journey. The admiration in the room was palpable, not just for his accomplishments but for the person he had become through those years of hard work, growth, and dedication. He was the true definition of professional success.

As the evening went on, I spoke with some of the younger professionals in the room, many of whom were just starting their own careers. Their excitement was contagious. They asked questions, sought advice, and shared their ambitions, each one of them eager to carve out their own path to success. Yet, I noticed something else—a sense of uncertainty. They wanted to succeed, but many of them were unsure of how to begin or what it would take to truly master their careers in today's fast-paced world.

It was in that moment, listening to their hopes and concerns, that the idea for this book began to take shape.

This book was written for those professionals. For the ones standing at the beginning of their journey, looking ahead with excitement but also uncertainty. It's for the people who want to be the best at what they do, who want to build a career that's more than just a series of promotions—it's a legacy of excellence, mastery, and meaningful connections.

Seeing how my mentor had left such a lasting impact on so many lives, I realized that professional success isn't just about what you achieve. It's about **how** you approach your career—how you develop the right skills, build strong relationships, and take control of your destiny.

Through years of experience and learning, I've discovered that success is not a singular destination. It's a journey of growth, intentional choices, and a willingness to learn at every stage. This book was created to offer insights, strategies, and practical advice to help you navigate that journey—whether you're just starting out, looking to advance, or hoping to reimagine your career.

The Keys to Career Mastery

In this book, we'll explore the core pillars of professional success:

- **Mastering essential skills**: In any profession, you must continuously sharpen and expand your skill set to stay relevant and valuable.
- **Building meaningful relationships**: No one succeeds alone. Relationships built on trust,

respect, and collaboration are critical to long-term success.
- **Taking ownership of your career**: Instead of waiting for opportunities to come to you, it's essential to create them, take initiative, and steer your career with intention.

This book isn't just about theories or trends—it's about providing actionable strategies that can be applied across professions. The lessons here are designed to empower you to take control of your professional journey, much like my mentor did, and build a career that reflects your highest aspirations.

You are the architect of your career. As you read, I hope you find inspiration and practical guidance that will help you master your craft, build lasting relationships, and achieve the kind of success that leaves an impact long after you've left the room.

So, let's begin the journey. Together, we'll discover the keys to unlocking your full potential and mastering the art of professional success.

DEFINING PROFESSIONAL SUCCESS

What is Professional Success?

The term **"professional success"** is something we often hear, but what does it really mean? Success, in any context, is a highly subjective term. To some, it may mean climbing the corporate ladder, while for others, it may mean maintaining a work-life balance while excelling in a chosen field. To truly understand professional success, we must break it down into two core components: **profession** and **success**.

A **profession** refers to a paid occupation that requires a particular set of skills and often involves formal training and qualifications. Whether it's teaching, law, engineering, or creative arts, the journey into any profession involves commitment, growth, and continuous learning.

Success, on the other hand, signifies the accomplishment of an aim or purpose. In the context of a profession, success can mean achieving specific career milestones—whether those involve promotions, recognition by peers, or reaching personal career goals. Success may also refer to the attainment of fame, wealth, or influence within a chosen profession. However, it's important to remember that success is not only measured by external standards but also by internal satisfaction and personal fulfillment.

Thus, **professional success** can be simply defined as the **attainment of success in one's chosen profession**. But it goes beyond that—professional success is about achieving more and more in your chosen profession through learning, honing, and practicing important skills, while also building meaningful relationships within a professional network. It involves constantly improving in your field, not just by focusing on personal development but by establishing lasting professional connections with customers, colleagues, managers, and peers.

The Components of Professional Success

Professional success is not an overnight phenomenon. It is the cumulative result of **skill development**, **relationship-building**, and **self-management**. These components, when honed and synchronized, lead to a sustainable and fulfilling career.

- **Achieving More**: Professional success is a continuous journey of achieving more over time. It involves not just performing your job but constantly finding ways to improve, adapt, and expand your skills and contributions. It is the act of stretching beyond the present comfort zone and aiming for growth. Success requires setting progressive goals—small and large—and relentlessly pursuing them.
- **Learning, Honing, and Practicing Skills**: No professional can reach success without mastering their craft. Skills need to be identified, developed, practiced, and refined continuously. This applies to both hard skills (technical knowledge specific to your profession) and soft skills (communication, leadership, teamwork, etc.). The more you sharpen your abilities, the more value you bring to your role, and the higher your chances of success.

- **Building Networks and Relationships**: Professional success does not occur in isolation. It is fostered through relationships—whether with colleagues, managers, subordinates, customers, or mentors. Networking is a fundamental part of building a career. These relationships open doors to opportunities, offer support and advice, and create a robust professional ecosystem. They contribute directly to how far and how quickly one can progress.

Success Defined by the Individual

While external achievements such as promotions, salary increases, or industry recognition may serve as benchmarks, the true essence of success lies in personal satisfaction. This form of success answers deeper questions: **Are you passionate about your work? Are you contributing to something meaningful? Are you constantly learning and growing?**

Professionals who focus solely on external achievements without considering personal fulfillment may find that, despite outward appearances of success, they feel unfulfilled or burnt out. Therefore, understanding and defining your own success is crucial. Some may define it as leadership positions, while others may see success in maintaining a balanced lifestyle while enjoying their work.

The Role of Values in Professional Success

An often-overlooked aspect of professional success is the alignment of your career with your personal values. If you value creativity but work in a highly structured and bureaucratic environment, success may feel hollow, even if you're moving up the ladder. Conversely, if your profession aligns with your values—whether they're about helping others, solving problems, or creating something new—you're more likely to feel that your career is a true success.

Take a moment to reflect on the following questions:

- **What do you value most in your work?**
- **What kind of legacy do you want to leave behind in your profession?**
- **How do you define success, both in terms of external achievements and internal satisfaction?**

By understanding what drives you, you can focus on career choices and paths that lead to both professional and personal fulfillment.

Success as a Journey, Not a Destination

One of the greatest misconceptions about success is that it is a fixed point, a finish line to cross. In reality, professional success is more accurately described as a journey—a dynamic and ongoing process that evolves as you grow in your career. There will be periods of rapid progress and times of stagnation or even setbacks, but it's essential to view success as a process of continuous growth, not a singular event.

Professionals who view success as a journey are more likely to adapt to challenges, stay motivated during difficult times, and find joy in the everyday process of learning and improving.

External and Internal Measures of Success

It's also important to differentiate between external and internal measures of success. **External measures** include things that others may judge you on—such as job titles, salaries, promotions, or public recognition. While these can be valuable indicators of progress, they are often beyond your control and may fluctuate due to external circumstances like market conditions or organizational changes.

Internal measures, on the other hand, are more personal and within your control. They include things like how much you enjoy your work, how meaningful you find your projects, and whether you feel you're learning and growing. Focusing on internal measures of success allows you to maintain motivation and satisfaction, even when external factors are unfavourable.

Professional Success Can Be You!

While professional success is often discussed in terms of continuous growth and skill development, it is also important to recognize that **professional success can refer to individuals who have attained significant success in their chosen professions**. These individuals have mastered their craft, built their reputation, and made notable contributions within their fields. Whether they are well-known public figures or professionals excelling quietly behind the scenes, their journey is marked by dedication, discipline, and mastery of their profession's core skills.

These successful professionals are often seen as role models, offering inspiration to others aspiring to similar success. Their stories underscore that professional success is not a one-size-fits-all journey—it can take many forms, depending on one's goals, values, and definitions of achievement.

This book aims to guide you to become a **professional success**.

The Three Key Components of Professional Success

As we explore the broader concept of professional success, it's essential to understand that achieving it relies on mastering three key components:

1. **Skill Development**: Every profession requires a specific set of skills. Whether technical or interpersonal, developing and refining these skills is foundational to professional success. This chapter introduces the concept of skill development, which will be explored further in the next chapter.
2. **Building and Sustaining Relationships**: Success doesn't occur in isolation. The ability to form strong, lasting relationships with colleagues, clients, mentors, and peers is crucial for advancing in any career. Relationship-building will be examined in detail later, but it plays a pivotal role in creating opportunities and support networks.
3. **Taking Ownership of Your Career**: Professional success is not just about skill and relationships—it's also about being proactive in managing your

career. This means taking responsibility for your growth, setting goals, and seeking out opportunities to advance. By taking control of your career trajectory, you ensure that your success is aligned with your personal and professional goals.

Leading into the Next Chapter: Skill Development

Now that we've explored the broad definition of professional success and its core components, it's time to dive deeper into the first and arguably the most critical component: **skill development**. Developing the right skills sets the foundation for a successful career, no matter the profession. In the next chapter, we will explore the importance of honing key skills, how to identify which skills are most relevant to your career, and practical strategies for continuous improvement.

Skill development is a continuous process, and it lays the groundwork for everything else. Whether you are just starting your career or are a seasoned professional looking to advance, understanding how to improve your skill set is essential to your long-term success.

SKILL DEVELOPMENT

The Foundation of Professional Success

Skill development is one of the cornerstones of professional success. No matter the industry or profession, having the right set of skills can significantly influence your career trajectory. In today's fast-paced world, where change is the only constant, the ability to adapt and learn new skills is essential for sustained success.

Skill development not only enhances your current capabilities but also prepares you for future challenges and opportunities. It allows you to stand out in a competitive job market and demonstrates your commitment to your profession. This chapter explores the critical aspects of skill development, including identifying necessary skills, honing them, and adopting effective learning strategies.

Identifying Necessary Skills

Before you can develop your skills, it's essential to identify which ones are relevant to your profession. Skills are often classified into two types: **hard skills** and **soft skills**.

- **Hard Skills**: These are particular, teachable abilities or knowledge bases that are typically measureable. Examples include coding, data analysis, graphic design, legal expertise, or technical proficiency in using industry-specific software. Acquiring hard skills typically involves traditional education, training programs, or practical experience.
- **Soft Skills**: Unlike hard skills, soft skills are more intangible and relate to how you interact with others and approach your work. They include appearance, communication, teamwork, problem-solving, interpersonal relations, leadership, and adaptability. Soft skills are increasingly recognized as vital to professional success, as they influence how you collaborate and navigate workplace dynamics.

Later in this chapter, we will discuss a few essential soft skills that cut across most professions, providing valuable insights and practical advice for developing these essential skills for professional success.

To identify the skills you need, consider the following steps:

1. **Research Your Field**: Look at job descriptions for positions you aspire to, noting the skills that are frequently mentioned.
2. **Seek Feedback**: Ask colleagues, mentors, or supervisors for input on which skills they believe are critical for success in your role.
3. **Self-Assessment**: Examinet your strengths and weaknesses. What are your strongest skills, and where could you improve?

Cultivating Skills Through Practice

Once you've identified the skills you need, the next step is to cultivate them through practice. Here are some effective strategies to enhance both hard and soft skills:

- **Engage in Continuous Learning**: Take advantage of online courses, workshops, webinars, and other training resources. Websites like Coursera, LinkedIn Learning, and Udemy offer a variety of courses tailored to different skills and industries.

- **Seek Mentorship**: Connect with experienced professionals in your field. A mentor can provide valuable insights, guidance, and feedback as you develop your skills. They can also share their own experiences and offer practical tips to help you navigate challenges.
- **Practice Deliberately**: For hard skills, practice is key. Whether you're coding, designing, or analyzing data, set aside dedicated time to practice your skills regularly. For soft skills, look for opportunities to engage in team projects or presentations that allow you to communicate, collaborate, and receive feedback.
- **Join Professional Associations**: Being part of professional organizations related to your field can provide access to resources, training, networking opportunities, and workshops that can aid in your skill development.
- **Volunteering and Side Projects**: Engaging in volunteer work or side projects allows you to apply your skills in real-world settings. This not only helps you refine your abilities but also demonstrates initiative and commitment to potential employers.

The Importance of Adaptability

In a world where technology and workplace dynamics are constantly evolving, the ability to adapt is more crucial than ever. This adaptability is a skill in itself. Professionals who can pivot, learn new technologies, and adjust to changing demands will be better positioned for success.

To cultivate adaptability, consider the following:

- **Stay Informed**: Regularly update yourself on industry trends, emerging technologies, and best practices. Subscribe to relevant newsletters, follow industry leaders on social media, and engage in discussions within your professional community.
- **Embrace Change**: Rather than viewing challenges and changes as obstacles, consider them opportunities for growth. Cultivating a positive mindset can make it easier to adapt to new circumstances.
- **Be Open to Feedback**: Actively seek constructive criticism and be willing to make adjustments based on feedback. This openness can help you develop resilience and enhance your skills.

Setting SMART Goals for Skill Development

A structured approach to skill development can make the process more effective. One popular method is to set **SMART goals**, which are:

- **Specific**: Clearly state your goals.
- **Measurable**: Decide how you will track progress.
- **Achievable**: Ensure your aim is realistic and reachable.
- **Relevant**: Align your goals with your long-term career objectives.
- **Time-Bound**: Set a timeline for reaching your goal.

SMART goals, for instance, would read something like this: "I will attend a public speaking workshop next month and practice by giving a presentation at work within three months." Rather than saying "I want to improve my public speaking skills,"

Tracking Your Progress

Monitoring your progress is vital for effective skill development. Regularly assess your growth and adjust your learning strategies as needed. Keeping a journal of your experiences, achievements, and challenges can provide valuable insights into your development journey.

You might also consider using a skills matrix, where you list your skills, rate your proficiency in each, and set goals for improvement. This structured approach not only keeps you accountable but also highlights areas where you've made significant progress.

A few fundamental Soft Skills

As we delve into the importance of soft skills, it's crucial to understand that these skills can significantly impact your professional success. This section will explore essential soft skills and provide practical advice for developing them.

Appearance: The Visual First Impression

Importance of a Professional Appearance
In the business world, first impressions are formed within seconds. A professional appearance is crucial as it sets the tone for how colleagues, clients, and superiors perceive you. Research indicates that people often make judgments about a person's competence, credibility, and professionalism based solely on their appearance. Therefore, dressing appropriately and maintaining a polished look can significantly influence how you are regarded in your professional environment.

How Personal Grooming and Dressing Affect Perceptions

Your attire and grooming habits communicate messages about your professionalism and attention to detail. For instance:

- **Dress Code Compliance**: Adhering to the dress code of your workplace not only demonstrates respect for the company culture but also signals your seriousness about your role. In environments where business casual is the norm, being too casual may give the impression that you lack professionalism.
- **Grooming**: Personal grooming, including cleanliness, hairstyle, and hygiene, affects how others perceive your competence and professionalism. A well-groomed person is frequently seen as more trustworthy and accountable.

Practical Tips

- **Understand Dress Codes**: Familiarize yourself with your workplace's dress code and choose outfits that fit appropriately. When in doubt, opt for slightly more formal attire than usual.

- **Grooming Habits**: Maintain regular grooming routines, such as haircuts, manicures, and skin care. Ensure that your clothing is neat, tidy, and ironed.
- **Organization**: Keep your workspace tidy and organized, as it reflects your overall professionalism. A neat workstation shows productivity and attention to detail.

Communication: The Key to Influence

Verbal, Non-Verbal, and Written Communication Skills
Effective communication is vital in the workplace, as it enables collaboration, reduces misunderstandings, and builds trust. It encompasses three main components:

- **Verbal Communication**: The words you choose, your tone, and your clarity all matter. Tailor your language to suit your audience, and ensure your message is clear and concise.
- **Non-Verbal Communication**: Includes body language, facial expressions, and eye contact, which all influence how your message is received. Confident body language can enhance your verbal messages and show engagement.

- **Written Communication**: Emails, reports, and memos should be clear, organized, and free of errors. Written communication is often the first impression of your professionalism, so it's crucial to present yourself effectively.

Strategies to Improve Communication Skills

- **Public Speaking**: Join organizations such as Toastmasters or take workshops that focus on developing public speaking skills. Practicing speeches in front of friends or family can also help ease anxiety.
- **Active Listening**: Practice active listening by giving your full attention during conversations, asking clarifying questions, and summarizing what the other person has said to ensure understanding.
- **Persuasive Writing**: Work on writing clearly and persuasively by focusing on structure and argument clarity. Read books on effective communication or enroll in a writing course.

Overcoming Shyness

- **Prepare and Practice**: If you're shy about speaking in meetings, prepare what you want to say ahead of time. To increase your confidence, rehearse your points.

- **Set Small Goals**: Start by speaking up in smaller group settings before addressing larger audiences. Gradually increase your participation to build comfort.

Telephone Etiquette: Representing Your Professionalism

Guidelines for Managing Professional Phone Calls
Telephone calls remain a vital aspect of business communication. Proper etiquette can ensure your professionalism is maintained:

- **Answer Promptly**: Greet the caller warmly and identify yourself and your company. For instance, "Good morning, you have reached [Your Company], my name is [Your Name]. How may I assist you?"
- **Be Polite and Respectful**: Always use polite language, and listen actively to the caller's needs. Refrain from interrupting and wait for them to complete speaking before answering.

Importance of Clear Communication
Clear communication is crucial, especially in professional settings. Make an effort to articulate your words and

maintain a moderate pace. If discussing complex topics, consider summarizing key points to ensure understanding.

Handling Difficult Conversations

- **Stay Calm**: Maintain composure during challenging discussions. Take deep breaths and speak slowly to manage your tone and avoid escalating the situation.
- **Empathize**: Acknowledge the caller's concerns and demonstrate understanding. To demonstrate empathy, say things like, "I understand your frustration."

Interpersonal Skills: Collaborating with Others

Building Strong, Collaborative Relationships

Interpersonal skills are vital for creating a positive workplace atmosphere.. Building strong relationships with colleagues can lead to better teamwork and job satisfaction. To build these relationships:

- **Engage in Team Activities**: Participate in team-building exercises or social events to strengthen connections.

- **Show Appreciation**: Acknowledge the contributions of others. Thank you notes and verbal appreciation are simple gestures that can help build rapport.

Navigating Conflicts and Fostering Teamwork
In any workplace, conflicts are unavoidable. Learning to navigate them effectively is crucial for maintaining relationships:

- **Address Issues Early**: Don't let conflicts fester. Look for areas of agreement while addressing conflicts constructively.
- **Encourage Open Dialogue**: Build an atmosphere in which team members feel comfortable discussing their ideas and concerns.. Open communication helps prevent misunderstandings.

The Value of Emotional Intelligence
Emotional intelligence (EI) is the ability to recognize and manage one's own emotions while empathizing with others. High EI can enhance teamwork and leadership. Key components include:

- **Self-Awareness**: Understand your emotions and how they influence the way you behave.

- **Self-Regulation**: Manage your emotions, especially in stressful situations, to respond thoughtfully rather than react impulsively.
- **Empathy**: Practice placing yourself in the shoes of others to better understand their emotions and views.

Leadership: Leading Before You're in Charge

Cultivating Leadership Skills

Effective leadership is not limited to those in management positions. Everyone can cultivate leadership skills:

- **Take Initiative**: Volunteer for projects or lead discussions in meetings, even if you're not the formal leader. This demonstrates your capability and willingness to take responsibility.
- **Empower Others**: Encourage colleagues by recognizing their strengths and providing opportunities for them to take on leadership roles within projects.

Building Trust and Leading by Example

In any kind of professional relationship, trust is essential. Develop trust by:

- **Being Consistent**: Follow through on commitments and be reliable in your actions.
- **Demonstrating Integrity**: Act ethically and transparently in all dealings, which encourages others to do the same.

Developing Decision-Making Skills

Strong decision-making skills are vital for effective leadership. To enhance these skills:

- **Analyze Information**: Gather relevant data before making decisions. Consider potential outcomes and impacts on your team.
- **Learn from Experience**: Consider your prior decisions—both good and bad. Understanding what worked and what didn't will help you make better decisions going forward.

Sales Skills: Selling Beyond Products

Influencing Ideas

Sales skills extend beyond selling products; they are about influencing ideas and building relationships. To be effective in this field:

- **Understand Your Audience**: Research the needs and preferences of your clients or colleagues. Tailor your approach to meet their individual situations.
- **Provide Solutions**: Focus on how your ideas or products can solve problems for others, rather than simply pitching what you offer.

Listening to Understand Others' Needs

Active listening is crucial in sales and professional interactions. Employ techniques such as:

- **Ask Open-Ended Questions**: Encourage others to share their thoughts and feelings to gain deeper insights into their needs.
- **Paraphrase and Summarize**: Reflect back what you've heard to demonstrate understanding and clarify any ambiguities.

Building Rapport with Clients and Colleagues

Strong relationships can lead to successful sales and collaborations. Tips for building rapport include:

- **Find Common Ground**: Look for shared interests or experiences to create connections.
- **Be Authentic**: Genuine interactions foster trust and make it easier to build lasting relationships.

Conclusion: A Lifelong Journey

Skill development is a continuous process and is vital for achieving professional success. Whether you are just starting your career or are a seasoned professional looking to advance, investing in your skills is essential to your long-term success. By identifying necessary skills, cultivating them through deliberate practice, and staying adaptable to changes in your field, you will build a solid foundation for your career.

As we move into the next chapter, we will explore the importance of building and sustaining relationships. Strong relationships are critical for networking, collaboration, and career advancement, and they complement the skills you've developed.

BUILDING MEANINGFUL RELATIONSHIPS

The Importance of Relationships in Professional Success

In any profession, relationships form the backbone of success. No matter how talented or skilled you are, your ability to build and maintain strong relationships with colleagues, clients, managers, and peers will significantly impact your career trajectory. Relationships are more than just social interactions—they are the currency of trust, support, and opportunity within any organization.

Building meaningful relationships isn't just about networking for personal gain. It's about creating authentic connections that foster trust, respect, and mutual benefit. In this chapter, we will explore how helping others, showing respect and appreciation, taking an interest in your coworkers, and practicing effective networking can lead to sustained professional success.

Helping Others: The Foundation of Trust

Helping others is one of the most fundamental ways to build trust in the workplace. When you assist others without expecting anything in return, it demonstrates that you are a team player who is invested in the success of the entire organization—not just your own career.

Offering help is not limited to grand gestures; it can be as simple as providing guidance to a colleague on a project, sharing your expertise with a new hire, or lending an extra hand when a team member is under pressure. These small acts of kindness accumulate over time and foster an environment of collaboration and reciprocity.

Practical Examples of Helping Others:

- **Offer assistance without being asked**: Take the initiative to help coworkers who may be struggling or overwhelmed, even if they haven't explicitly asked for it.

- **Be specific in your offer**: Instead of saying, "Let me know if you need help," be proactive and suggest ways you can assist, such as, "I noticed you're working on that report. Would you like me to help with the data analysis?"
- **Share resources**: If you come across an article, tool, or contact that could help someone in their work, don't hesitate to share it.

By consistently helping others, you not only build trust but also position yourself as a valuable team member and leader, which can lead to greater opportunities for growth and advancement.

Respect and Appreciation: Keys to Positive Work Environments

Respect and appreciation are the cornerstones of any successful relationship, and they are particularly vital in the workplace. A positive work environment thrives when individuals respect one another's roles, contributions, and differences. Showing appreciation, even for small tasks, can significantly improve team morale, foster stronger relationships, and create a culture where people feel valued and motivated.

How to Show Respect and Appreciation:

- **Respect every role**: No matter someone's position, from entry-level employees to senior executives, their role is critical to the overall success of the company. Treat everyone with equal respect, regardless of their title.
- **Acknowledge the efforts of others**: Don't wait for someone to complete a large project to show appreciation. Recognize the smaller, everyday contributions that keep things running smoothly.
- **Give specific praise**: When showing appreciation, be specific. Instead of simply saying, "Great job," say, "I really valued the way you handled that customer call—it was crucial in resolving the issue."

Handling Mistakes with Respect: Even when someone makes a mistake, it's important to approach the situation with respect. Instead of focusing on what went wrong, acknowledge the person's effort, then offer constructive guidance on how they can improve. By being respectful in your feedback, you encourage growth and learning rather than creating resentment.

Taking an Interest: Connecting Beyond Work

While professionalism is important, it's equally critical to recognize that your colleagues and coworkers are individuals with lives, interests, and experiences outside of work. Taking an interest in your colleagues as people—not just as coworkers—can go a long way in building strong, lasting relationships.

Why Personal Connections Matter:

- **Increases Trust**: When people feel that you genuinely care about them, they are more likely to trust you and work closely with you.
- **Strengthens Teamwork**: Personal connections can enhance collaboration and teamwork, as people are more willing to help and support those they have a deeper connection with.
- **Fosters Loyalty**: Showing interest in the well-being and personal life of your coworkers can build loyalty and make your work environment more enjoyable.

How to Take an Interest in Your Colleagues:

- **Ask about their interests**: Instead of jumping straight into work discussions, take a moment to ask your colleagues how their weekend was, or inquire about their hobbies or family. Small conversations like this can strengthen relationships.
- **Remember details**: If someone mentions something significant, like a family event or personal achievement, follow up later to ask how it

went. This shows that you were listening and genuinely care.
- **Listen more, talk less**: While it's good to share about yourself, focus more on listening to your colleagues. This allows you to understand them better and make meaningful connections.

By taking an interest in your coworkers, you foster a work environment based on empathy and respect, which in turn leads to stronger, more collaborative relationships.

Networking: Expanding Your Professional Circle

While networking is often seen as a career advancement tool, it is fundamentally about building relationships. Expanding your professional network within and outside your organization can open up new opportunities, provide you with valuable advice and support, and help you grow in your career.

Networking is more than just exchanging business cards and building superficial connections. Instead, it's about establishing relationships that are mutually beneficial and based on genuine interest.

Effective Networking Strategies:

- **Be open and approachable**: Whether at networking events or in casual work settings, make an effort to engage with people. Approach new contacts with openness, authenticity, and a willingness to learn about their work and experiences.
- **Have a plan, but be flexible**: When attending networking events, have an idea of the types of connections you'd like to make, but be open to unexpected conversations and opportunities.
- **Follow up**: The first meeting is just the beginning of networking. Follow up with contacts you've made, whether through a simple thank-you note, a LinkedIn connection, or an invitation to continue the conversation over coffee. Regular follow-up demonstrates your appreciation for the relationship.

Building and Maintaining Relationships:

- **Offer value**: Networking should not be one-sided. Offer value to your connections by sharing insights, providing introductions, or helping them with their own goals.
- **Keep in touch**: Maintain your relationships by periodically checking in, even if you don't need

anything. This could be as simple as sending a congratulatory message for a new job or forwarding an interesting article relevant to their industry.

By practicing effective networking, you can build a strong professional support system that can offer guidance, advice, and opportunities throughout your career.

Conclusion: Relationships as a Cornerstone of Success

Building meaningful relationships is a vital aspect of professional success. Whether you're helping others, showing respect and appreciation, taking an interest in your colleagues, or networking to expand your professional circle, these interactions lay the foundation for a successful and fulfilling career.

Strong relationships don't just create opportunities—they foster collaboration, trust, and a positive work environment, all of which are essential for long-term success.

As we move into the next chapter, we'll explore how taking control of your career by setting goals, asking for what you need, and staying motivated will help you continue on the path to professional success.

TAKING CONTROL OF YOUR CAREER

Owning Your Journey to Success

Taking control of your career means being proactive about your professional growth. It's about recognizing that your success isn't determined solely by your employer, manager, or external circumstances but by the decisions you make and the actions you take. While your organization can provide opportunities, it's ultimately up to you to seize them, chart your path, and ensure that you're continuously moving forward in your career.

In this chapter, we will explore how taking responsibility, learning the power of asking, staying self-motivated, and demonstrating dedication can help you take ownership of your career and steer it in the direction of your goals.

Taking Responsibility: Own Your Journey

One of the most important aspects of taking control of your career is **accountability**. Taking responsibility for both your successes and failures is essential to professional growth. When you own your actions, you gain the power to learn from them and make informed decisions about your future.

Why Accountability Matters

- **Accepting Mistakes**: Everyone makes mistakes, but how you respond to them shapes your career. Instead of shifting blame, acknowledge what went wrong, learn from the experience, and move forward with solutions.
- **Owning Your Success**: Just as it's important to own your mistakes, you should also take pride in your achievements. Don't downplay your successes; recognize them as evidence of your hard work and growth.

Ways to Take Responsibility in Your Career:

- **Set Personal Goals**: Establish clear professional goals that align with your values and aspirations. By setting and tracking your goals, you take responsibility for your own development.
- **Seek Feedback**: Don't wait for annual reviews to ask for feedback. Actively seek input from supervisors, peers, and mentors to understand where you can improve and how you can better contribute to your team.
- **Reflect on Your Progress**: Take the time to assess your growth on a regular basis. What have you accomplished? Where have you fallen short? What steps can you take to get back on track or move closer to your long-term goals?

Taking responsibility empowers you to control your career narrative, ensuring that you're not passively waiting for opportunities but actively creating them.

The Power of Asking: Opportunities, Help, and Feedback

Being proactive also involves mastering the art of asking. Many professionals hesitate to ask for what they need—whether it's opportunities, help, or feedback—out of fear of rejection, appearing incompetent, or seeming overconfident. However, asking is an essential skill that can open doors and lead to career advancement.

Why Asking Is Important

- **Unlocks Opportunities**: Asking for more responsibility or additional projects can signal to your employer that you're ready for growth. It positions you as a proactive, ambitious employee.
- **Builds Relationships**: Asking for advice or help strengthens relationships with colleagues and mentors. It demonstrates humility and a readiness to learn from others.
- **Clarifies Expectations**: If you're unclear about your role, goals, or feedback, asking can provide the clarity you need to stay aligned with your objectives and your organization's expectations.

How to Ask Effectively:

- **Be Specific**: When asking for opportunities, help, or feedback, be clear about what you need. For example, instead of asking, "Can you give me feedback on my work?" you could ask, "Can you give me specific feedback on how I handled the client presentation last week?"
- **Demonstrate Initiative**: When asking for additional responsibilities or projects, show how they align

with your career goals. Frame it as a way for you to contribute more effectively to the team.
- **Be Respectful of Others' Time**: When asking for help or advice, acknowledge that the person you're asking may be busy. Be considerate and give them the space to provide thoughtful responses.

The willingness to ask is not a sign of weakness—it's a sign of growth. It shows that you're eager to learn, develop, and seize opportunities for advancement.

Self-Motivation: The Drive to Succeed

Success doesn't come to those who wait passively for it. **Self-motivation** is the fuel that drives you to consistently seek new challenges, improve your skills, and achieve your goals. While external factors like recognition or financial rewards can be motivating, intrinsic motivation—driven by a personal desire to grow and succeed—is far more powerful.

How to Cultivate Self-Motivation:

- **Set Clear, Achievable Goals**: Setting realistic, incremental goals provides direction and a sense of purpose. Break larger career objectives into smaller, manageable tasks to maintain momentum.

- **Find Meaning in Your Work**: Connect your daily tasks to your long-term career goals or personal values. Understanding how your work contributes to the bigger picture can increase your commitment and enthusiasm.
- **Challenge Yourself Regularly**: Constantly seek out new challenges. Whether it's learning a new skill, leading a project, or taking on more responsibility, pushing your limits prevents complacency and keeps you engaged.
- **Celebrate Your Wins**: Recognize your achievements—both big and small. Celebrating progress, no matter how incremental, reinforces a positive mindset and motivates you to continue striving for more.

Self-motivation means staying driven even when things get tough. It's about being your own advocate, recognizing that you are responsible for your own success.

Dedication: The Long Road to Success

Professional success is not an overnight event—it's the result of dedication, persistence, and determination over time. Dedication requires a deep commitment to your goals, along with the resilience to overcome setbacks and challenges.

Understanding Dedication:

- **Consistency Is Key**: Dedication is about showing up consistently and putting in the effort day after day, even when progress feels slow. Whether it's working through challenges, continuing to improve your skills, or staying the course when things are difficult, persistence pays off.
- **Delayed Gratification**: Real success often involves delayed gratification. You may not see immediate rewards for your efforts, but staying focused on your long-term goals can lead to more significant achievements down the road.
- **Balancing Short- and Long-Term Goals**: Dedication involves balancing your daily tasks with your broader career objectives. While it's important to excel in your current role, keep your long-term goals in mind and make time to work toward them as well.

Taking control of your career means being proactive about your professional growth. It's about recognizing that your success isn't determined solely by your employer, manager, or external circumstances but by the decisions you make and the actions you take. While your organization can provide opportunities, it's ultimately up to you to seize them, chart your path, and ensure that you're continuously moving forward in your career.

In this chapter, we will explore how taking responsibility, learning the power of asking, staying self-motivated, and demonstrating dedication can help you take ownership of your career and steer it in the direction of your goals.

Taking Responsibility: Own Your Journey

One of the most important aspects of taking control of your career is **accountability**. Taking responsibility for both your successes and failures is essential to professional growth. When you own your actions, you gain the power to learn from them and make informed decisions about your future.

Why Accountability Matters

- **Accepting Mistakes**: Everyone makes mistakes, but how you respond to them shapes your career. Instead of shifting blame, acknowledge what went wrong, learn from the experience, and move forward with solutions.
- **Owning Your Success**: Just as it's important to own your mistakes, you should also take pride in your achievements. Don't downplay your

successes; recognize them as evidence of your hard work and growth.

Ways to Take Responsibility in Your Career:

- **Set Personal Goals**: Establish clear professional goals that align with your values and aspirations. By setting and tracking your goals, you take responsibility for your own development.
- **Seek Feedback**: Don't wait for annual reviews to ask for feedback. Actively seek input from supervisors, peers, and mentors to understand where you can improve and how you can better contribute to your team.
- **Reflect on Your Progress**: Take the time to assess your growth on a regular basis. What have you accomplished? Where have you fallen short? What steps can you take to get back on track or move closer to your long-term goals?

Taking responsibility empowers you to control your career narrative, ensuring that you're not passively waiting for opportunities but actively creating them.

The Power of Asking: Opportunities, Help, and Feedback

Being proactive also involves mastering the art of asking. Many professionals hesitate to ask for what they need—whether it's opportunities, help, or feedback—out of fear of rejection, appearing incompetent, or seeming overconfident. However, asking is an essential skill that can open doors and lead to career advancement.

Why Asking Is Important

- **Unlocks Opportunities**: Asking for more responsibility or additional projects can signal to your employer that you're ready for growth. It positions you as a proactive, ambitious employee.
- **Builds Relationships**: Asking for advice or help strengthens relationships with colleagues and mentors. It demonstrates humility and a readiness to learn from others.
- **Clarifies Expectations**: If you're unclear about your role, goals, or feedback, asking can provide the clarity you need to stay aligned with your objectives and your organization's expectations.

How to Ask Effectively:

- **Be Specific**: When asking for opportunities, help, or feedback, be clear about what you need. For example, instead of asking, "Can you give me feedback on my work?" you could ask, "Can you give me specific feedback on how I handled the client presentation last week?"
- **Demonstrate Initiative**: When asking for additional responsibilities or projects, show how they align with your career goals. Frame it as a way for you to contribute more effectively to the team.
- **Be Respectful of Others' Time**: When asking for help or advice, acknowledge that the person you're asking may be busy. Be considerate and give them the space to provide thoughtful responses.

The willingness to ask is not a sign of weakness—it's a sign of growth. It shows that you're eager to learn, develop, and seize opportunities for advancement.

Self-Motivation: The Drive to Succeed

Success doesn't come to those who wait passively for it. **Self-motivation** is the fuel that drives you to consistently seek new challenges, improve your skills, and achieve your goals. While external factors like recognition or financial rewards can be motivating, intrinsic motivation—driven by a personal desire to grow and succeed—is far more powerful.

How to Cultivate Self-Motivation:

- **Set Clear, Achievable Goals**: Setting realistic, incremental goals provides direction and a sense of purpose. Break larger career objectives into smaller, manageable tasks to maintain momentum.
- **Find Meaning in Your Work**: Connect your daily tasks to your long-term career goals or personal values. Understanding how your work contributes to the bigger picture can increase your commitment and enthusiasm.
- **Challenge Yourself Regularly**: Constantly seek out new challenges. Whether it's learning a new skill, leading a project, or taking on more responsibility, pushing your limits prevents complacency and keeps you engaged.
- **Celebrate Your Wins**: Recognize your achievements—both big and small. Celebrating progress, no matter how incremental, reinforces a positive mindset and motivates you to continue striving for more.

Self-motivation means staying driven even when things get tough. It's about being your own advocate, recognizing that you are responsible for your own success.

Dedication: The Long Road to Success

Professional success is not an overnight event—it's the result of dedication, persistence, and determination over time. Dedication requires a deep commitment to your goals, along with the resilience to overcome setbacks and challenges.

Understanding Dedication:

- **Consistency Is Key**: Dedication is about showing up consistently and putting in the effort day after day, even when progress feels slow. Whether it's working through challenges, continuing to improve your skills, or staying the course when things are difficult, persistence pays off.
- **Delayed Gratification**: Real success often involves delayed gratification. You may not see immediate rewards for your efforts, but staying focused on your long-term goals can lead to more significant achievements down the road.
- **Balancing Short- and Long-Term Goals**: Dedication involves balancing your daily tasks with your broader career objectives. While it's important to excel in your current role, keep your long-term goals in mind and make time to work toward them as well.

CONCLUSION

The Continuous Journey of Professional Success

As we've explored throughout this book, professional success is not a one-time achievement or a finish line to cross—it is an ongoing journey. This journey is shaped by your dedication to mastering your craft, building meaningful relationships, and taking ownership of your career. It's about making deliberate choices, learning from experiences, and evolving as both a professional and a person.

In each chapter, we have examined different components of professional success, from developing the right skills to building strong relationships and embracing the mindset of continuous growth. As we conclude, it's essential to tie these elements together and reflect on how they interconnect to form a cohesive path toward a fulfilling and successful career.

Skill Development: The Foundation of Success

At the heart of professional success is **skill development**. Whether you are refining hard skills—such as technical proficiency, data analysis, or industry-specific knowledge—or soft skills—like communication, leadership, and emotional intelligence—continuous learning is essential.

The world of work is always changing, with new technologies, methods, and expectations emerging constantly. By committing to lifelong learning, you ensure that you stay adaptable, competitive, and capable of taking on new challenges. The more you invest in your skills, the more value you bring to your organization, colleagues, and clients.

As you advance in your career, continue to:

- **Identify areas for growth**: Regularly assess where you can improve or expand your expertise.

- **Engage in deliberate practice**: Set aside time to practice and refine your skills.
- **Seek out new learning opportunities**: Attend workshops, pursue certifications, or engage in self-directed learning.

Skill development is the foundation upon which your professional success is built, and it is an ongoing process that never truly ends.

Building and Sustaining Relationships: The Key to Collaboration

No matter how skilled or talented you are, your ability to **build and sustain relationships** will greatly influence your success. Relationships provide support, guidance, opportunities, and collaboration. Whether it's helping others, showing appreciation, or expanding your professional network, relationships form the core of a positive and successful work environment.

Throughout your career, you will interact with colleagues, managers, clients, and mentors. Each relationship presents an opportunity for growth, learning, and support. Strong professional relationships can lead to promotions, career changes, and collaborations that drive success.

To continue cultivating meaningful relationships:

- **Be intentional in your interactions**: Take the time to understand others, offer support, and build trust.
- **Practice active listening and empathy**: Take sincere interest in the viewpoints and experiences of others.
- **Maintain your network**: Regularly check in with your professional contacts, and nurture your relationships over time.

A successful career is not built in isolation—it thrives on collaboration, trust, and mutual respect. Your ability to form and sustain meaningful relationships will enhance both your personal satisfaction and professional achievements.

Taking Ownership of Your Career: The Power of Self-Management

Perhaps the most empowering realization in your professional journey is that **you are in control of your career**. While external factors like your organization or industry may influence your path, it is ultimately your decisions, actions, and mindset that determine your success.

In Chapter 4, we explored how taking responsibility, setting SMART goals, asking for what you need, and staying motivated are all essential to self-management. These principles give you the power to create opportunities and achieve the success you desire.

As you move forward, remember:

- **Own your growth**: Take responsibility for your actions, learn from mistakes, and celebrate your successes.
- **Be proactive**: Don't wait for opportunities—create them by asking for feedback, seeking new responsibilities, and stepping outside your comfort zone.
- **Stay motivated**: Keep your long-term goals in mind, and maintain the drive to push through challenges. Stay focused on the bigger picture, even when day-to-day tasks become overwhelming.

Taking control of your career means being both the architect and the builder of your professional success. By embracing self-management, you ensure that you are actively shaping your future.

The Bigger Picture: Success Beyond External Achievements

While external achievements—such as promotions, raises, or recognition—are important markers of success, true professional fulfillment often comes from within. It is essential to remember that success is not only about what you accomplish, but also about the impact you have, the relationships you build, and the personal growth you experience along the way.

- **Personal Fulfillment**: True success is measured by how aligned your career is with your values, passions, and goals. Are you doing work that you find meaningful? Are you continuously growing and learning? Does your career provide you with personal satisfaction as well as external rewards?
- **Legacy and Impact**: As you continue to progress in your career, consider the legacy you are leaving behind. What do you want to be known for? How have you made a positive impact on those around you? Whether it's through mentoring others, contributing to your industry, or fostering a supportive work environment, your impact can be a lasting measure of success.

The Path Forward: A Call to Action

Professional success is a journey that requires effort, commitment, and adaptability. As you reflect on the lessons in this book, consider the actionable steps you can take to continue your journey:

1. **Develop Your Skills**: Identify key areas for improvement and commit to continuous learning.
2. **Foster Relationships**: Build meaningful, collaborative relationships with colleagues, mentors, and peers.
3. **Own Your Career**: Take responsibility for your growth, seek out opportunities, and stay motivated.
4. **Define Your Success**: Recognize that true success goes beyond external validation—it's about personal fulfillment and the positive impact you create.

Embrace the Journey

The path to professional success is not linear, nor is it without its challenges. However, by embracing this journey with a growth mindset, a commitment to learning, and a willingness to take ownership of your future, you can create a career that is not only successful but also deeply fulfilling.

Your journey is unique, and the choices you make will define your path. Stay curious, keep learning, and remember that success is a continuous process—one that evolves as you do.

As you move forward, take these lessons with you and strive for a career that reflects your values, aspirations, and vision for the future. Professional success is not just a destination—it's the journey you choose to take every day.

About the Author

Israel J. Abifarin is a passionate professional with over two decades of experience in Sales, Marketing and Business Development. Throughout his career, Israel has mentored countless individuals, helping them master essential skills, build meaningful relationships, and take charge of their careers. His approach to professional success combines real-world insights with practical strategies, making him a trusted guide for anyone seeking long-term career growth.

With a commitment to lifelong learning, Israel has dedicated his career to empowering others to unlock their full potential. **Professional Success: Discovering the Keys to Career Mastery** reflects his deep belief that true success comes from not only achieving personal goals but also leaving a lasting impact on the professional world.